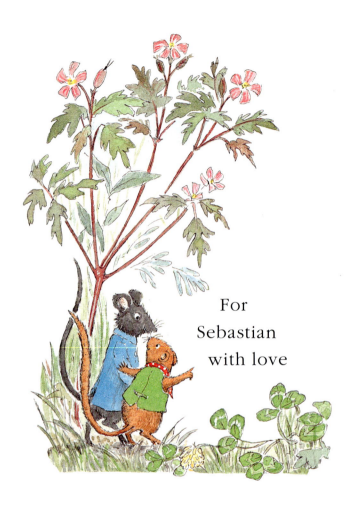

For
Sebastian
with love

First published 1992 by Walker Books Ltd
87 Vauxhall Walk, London SE11 5HJ

This edition published 1999

2 4 6 8 10 9 7 5 3 1

This book has been typeset in Garamond.

Printed in Singapore

British Library Cataloguing in Publication Data
A catalogue record for this book is
available from the British Library.

ISBN 0-7445-6777-7 (hb)
ISBN 0-7445-7223-1 (pb)

THIS WALKER BOOK BELONGS TO:

THE TOWN MOUSE AND THE COUNTRY MOUSE

HELEN CRAIG

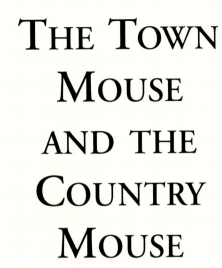

WALKER BOOKS
AND SUBSIDIARIES

LONDON • BOSTON • SYDNEY

Once upon a time, deep in the hedgerow, there lived a country mouse called Charlie. One afternoon, he was sitting at his window listening to a blackbird singing while the sun warmed the fur on his back, when suddenly there was a knock at the door. It was his cousin, Tyler the town mouse.

"Hello there, Charlie! I've come to visit," said Tyler, marching in and flopping down in Charlie's best armchair. "I'm exhausted. What a journey! Got anything to eat?"

Charlie fetched him a bowl of nuts and marigold seeds topped with some red hawthorn berries he had been saving for a special treat. But Tyler wrinkled his nose. "What plain food," he said. "Still, I suppose it's good for you."

When he had finished eating, he leant back. "Now, Charlie, is there anything going on around here in the evenings?" Charlie smiled. "Yes, there is. I'll take you to see something wonderful."

That evening they climbed the hill behind Charlie's house.
The sun was just going down and all the birds were singing their best songs. They waited while the sky filled with brilliant colours.
"There!" whispered Charlie.
"Where?" said Tyler.

"The sunset," said Charlie.
"Isn't it beautiful?"
Tyler yawned. "Too slow
for me. I like a bit of action."
And he set off down the hill.

That night, Tyler couldn't sleep. The countryside was just too dark and quiet.

Next morning, when he saw that breakfast was nuts, seeds and berries again, he decided enough was enough.

"Sorry, Charlie," he said. "Country life is not for me. I need the bright lights of the town. But why don't you come back with me and see how exciting life can be?"

Charlie had never been further than the top of the hill, but he said bravely, "All right, I will. Just let me pack a few things." And they set off.

They had not gone far when they met a carrier pigeon. "I'm on my way to town," she said. "Would you like a lift? Climb aboard and hold on tight!"

To
TOWN
10
MILE?

As they soared high into the air, Charlie watched his hedgerow get smaller and smaller until it disappeared. He felt quite lost.

It was a long journey. At last the carrier pigeon set them down in the town market-place. Charlie stood rooted to the spot. There were so many people; there was so much noise.

"Come on, Charlie," hissed Tyler, dragging him into the safety of the shadows.

"It's dangerous here. Stick close and follow me."

They scuttled off, along a gutter,

across a pavement,

up an iron staircase,

over rooftops,

down a chimney,

and through a window.

At the end of a musty passage, bright light streamed from a small hole.

"In we go," whispered Tyler and he squeezed through. Charlie followed.

Aaaah! A giant cat with fierce eyes and huge sharp teeth was waiting to pounce on them! "**Help!**" squealed Charlie.

He swayed and fell, but Tyler caught him by the tail. He was laughing. "Don't be silly, Charlie, we're in a cinema. It's only a film."

Poor Charlie peeped through his paws. The giant cat was now chasing a giant mouse. It was all very strange.

The film ended and they set off again through the dark streets. On the way Charlie nearly got squashed…

gassed…

drowned in a sea of paper…

and knocked out by a runaway pineapple.

"You must be more careful!" said Tyler, picking him up for the fourth time.

Charlie was very glad when they reached the steps of the big house where Tyler lived.

"I expect you're hungry," said Tyler leading the way to the dining-room. "Let's see what's left." And he dashed round the table looking for the best bits. "Have some sardines and chocolate mousse," he said.

"How about prawns in mayonnaise or prunes and custard?"

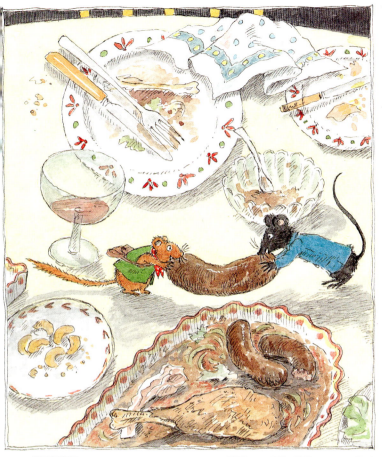

He offered Charlie sausages,
ice-cream and a bit of
fatty bacon.

"Have a drink!" he called,
knocking over a wine glass.
Charlie didn't like any of
it much. He was beginning
to feel very sick and dizzy.

Suddenly there was a horrible noise.
Yeowwoull!
Thump!
Crash!
A fat cat landed on the table.
Tyler vanished.

YEOWWOULL!

The cat sprang.
Charlie jumped.

The cat chased him round and round and up and down,

until Charlie dived under a sofa and scuttled up into one of the springs.

The cat could smell Charlie. Charlie could smell the cat. The cat watched the sofa for a long, long time. Charlie waited, trembling. He thought his end had come and he would never see his comfortable home in the hedgerow again.

At last he heard the cat being
shooed out and almost at once
Tyler appeared.

"Sorry, Charlie. Forgot to tell you
where the mouse hole was. Are
you all right? You look a bit odd."

And he led Charlie to his home
under the sideboard and put
him to bed.

Charlie had nightmares all night.

Very early in the
morning he woke
Tyler and said,
"I'm sorry, town life
is just too much
for me. I think I'd
better go home."

So Tyler took him
back to the market-
place and put him
on a milk van that
was going to the farm
near the hedgerow.

Charlie was so pleased
to be home again. He
ate a large dish of red
hawthorn berries while
the blackbird sang and
the sun warmed the
fur on his back.

That night Tyler put on his top hat, white tie and tails and set off across town for some fun at the theatre. He was very happy.

Under the same night sky, Charlie lay on his hill. He had watched the sun set and now he was counting the stars. He was very happy too!

MORE WALKER PAPERBACKS
For You to Enjoy

CHARLIE AND TYLER AT THE SEASIDE
by Helen Craig

In this new adventure for the town mouse and the country mouse,
Charlie and Tyler go on a trip to the seaside, and have a very exciting day indeed!

"Helen Craig's mouse duo make a welcome return … wonderfully atmospheric to read aloud."
Julie Myerson, The Mail on Sunday

0-7445-7224-X   £4.99

THE VERY BEST OF AESOP'S FABLES
by Margaret Clark/Charlotte Voake

Shortlisted for the Kurt Maschler Award, this is an entertaining selection of
eleven of the most popular of Aesop's classic tales – without the morals.

"Bright as new paint… Clear, snappy and sharp, yet retains all the elegance and point of the originals.
Delicately illustrated by the inimitable Charlotte Voake." *The Sunday Times*

0-7445-3149-7   £5.99

MARY MARY
by Sarah Hayes/Helen Craig

Formerly on the list of texts to be used in conjunction with the
Standard Assessment Tasks of the National Curriculum (Key Stage 2, Level 1 – 2),
this is the original tale of a shambolic giant and the small girl who sorts him out.

"This fairy tale has a friendly giant and an intrepid heroine,
two excellent ingredients for a winning story." *Child Education*

0-7445-2062-2   £4.99